BENIN

BENIN

LORDS OF THE RIVER

PHILIP KOSLOW

CHELSEA HOUSE PUBLISHERS • New York • Philadelphia

Frontispiece: A 17th-century bronze plaque depicting a group of officials serving in the royal palace of Benin.

On the Cover: An artist's interpretation of a bronze head from Benin; in the background, a royal procession moves through the streets of 17th-century Benin City.

CHELSEA HOUSE PUBLIHERS
Editorial Director Richard Rennert
Executive Managing Editor Karyn Gullen Browne
Copy Chief Robin James
Picture Editor Adrian G. Allen
Creative Editor Robert Mitchell
Art Director Joan Ferrigno
Production Manager Sallye Scott

THE KINGDOMS OF AFRICA
Senior Editor Martin Schwabacher

Staff for Benin
Assistant Editor Catherine Iannone
Editorial Assistant Erin McKenna
Senior Designer Cambraia Magalhães
Picture Researcher Ellen Dudley
Cover Illustrator Bradford Brown

First Printing
1 3 5 7 9 8 6 4 2

Library of Congress Cataloging-in-Publication Data

Koslow, Philip.
  Benin : lords of the river   Philip Koslow.
    p. cm.—(The Kingdoms of Africa)
Includes bibliographical references and index.
  ISBN   0-7910-3133-0.
         0-7910-3134-9 (pbk.)
    1. Benin (Nigeria)—Civilization—Juvenile literature. 2. Benin (Nigeria)—History—Juvenile literature. [1. Benin (Nigeria)—History. 2. Bini (African people)] I. Title. II. Series.   95-12343
DT515.9.B37K67 1995   CIP
966.9'32—dc20   AC

CONTENTS

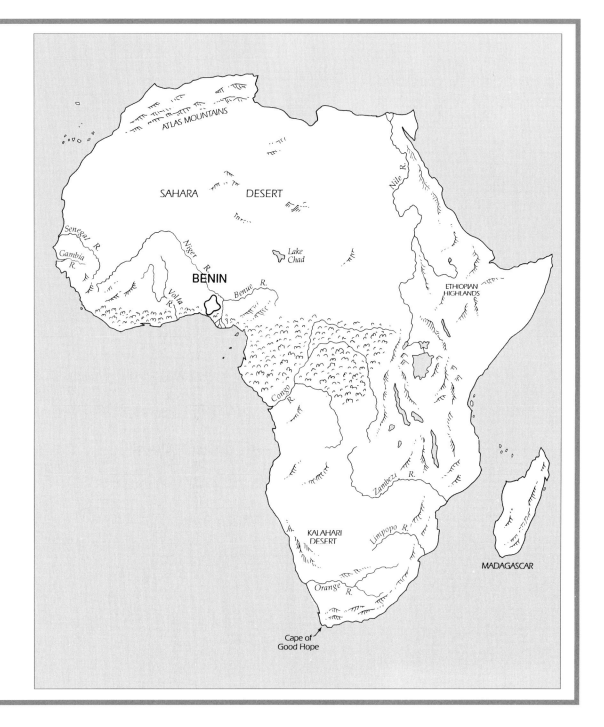

"CIVILIZATION AND MAGNIFICENCE"

On a sunny morning in July 1796, Mungo Park, a Scottish doctor turned explorer, achieved a major goal of his long and difficult trek through West Africa when he reached the banks of the mighty Niger River. Along the river was a cluster of four large towns, which together made up the city of Segu, the principal settlement of the Bambara people. The sight of Segu dazzled Park as much as the spectacle of the broad, shining waterway. "The view of this extensive city," he wrote, "the numerous canoes upon the river; the crowded population; and the cultivated state of the surrounding country, formed altogether a prospect of civilization and magnificence, which I little expected to find in the bosom of Africa."

7

Park's account of his journey, *Travels in the Interior Districts of Africa*, became a best-seller in England. But his positive reflections on Africa were soon brushed aside by the English and other Europeans, who were engaged in a profitable trade in slaves along the West African coast and were eventually to carve up the entire continent into colonies. Later explorers such as Richard Burton, who spoke of the "childishness" and "backwardness" of Africans, achieved more lasting fame than did Park, who drowned during a second expedition to Africa in 1806. Thus it is not surprising that 100 years after Park's arrival at Segu, a professor at England's Oxford University could write with bland self-assurance that African history before the arrival of Europeans had been nothing more than "blank, uninteresting, brutal barbarism." The professor's opinion was published when the British Empire was at its height, and it represented a point of view that was necessary to justify the exploitation of Africans. If, as the professor claimed, Africans had lived in a state of chaos throughout their history, then their European conquerors

A relief map of Africa, indicating the territory once controlled by the kingdom of Benin.

This head of an oba (king) from 18th-century Benin is one of the countless great artworks produced by the peoples of Africa before European powers began to dominate the continent during the late 19th century.

could believe that they were doing a noble deed by imposing their will and their way of life upon Africa's people.

The colonialist view of African history held sway into the 20th century. But as Africans gained their independence from the European powers, more enlightened scholars began to take a fresh look at Africa's past. As archaeologists (scientists who study the physical remains of past societies) explored the sites of former African cities, they found that Africans had enjoyed a high level of civilization hundreds of years before the arrival of Europeans. In many respects, the kingdoms and cities of Africa had been equal to or more advanced than European societies during the same period.

Modern scientists also reject the idea—fostered by Europeans during the time of the slave trade and colonialism—that there is any connection between a people's skin color and their capacity for achievement and self-government. Differences in pigmentation, scientists now recognize, are based solely upon climate and have nothing to do with intellectual ability. When the human species began to develop in the torrid regions of Africa some 7.5 million years ago, humans were all dark skinned because dark pigmentation protected them from the harmful ultraviolet rays of the sun. However, when some Africans began migrating to colder regions where there was far less sunlight, heavy pigmentation became a drawback—it prevented the skin from absorbing the amount of sunlight needed to produce vitamin D, which is essential for the growth of bones and teeth. Hence lighter skin began to predominate in Europe, with the peoples of Asia, the Middle East, and North Africa occupying a middle ground between Europeans and dark-skinned Africans. Rather than indicating superiority, therefore, lighter skin can be viewed as a deviance from the original skin color of all human beings.

As early as the 5th century B.C., when ancient Greece was enjoying its Golden Age, West African peoples had developed a highly civilized way of life and were producing magnificent works of art. By A.D. 750, ancient Ghana, known as the Land of Gold, emerged as West Africa's first centralized kingdom. When Ghana began to decline in the 12th century, power shifted to the empire of Mali, and Mali was in turn supplanted by Songhay, Kanem-Borno, and the fortress kingdoms of Hausaland. All these great nations were located in the central region of West Africa—the wide, sun-baked savanna that borders the vast Sahara Desert. To a large extent, they owed their wealth and grandeur to trade with North Africa and the Middle East. Because of this ever-widening economic and cultural contact, the fame of the Bilad al-Sudan ("land of the black peoples" in Arabic) spread throughout the world.

However, the rich saga of the savanna states does not represent the entire history of West African achievement. Indeed, much of the region's wealth derived from the gold and ivory supplied by the peoples of the lush forest belt that extends along the southern coast of West Africa. The forestland communities had emerged at least as early as those of the savanna, but their distant location and rugged terrain ensured that they would be known to few outsiders before the arrival of European mariners in the 15th century. Their history forms a unique chapter in the development of African civilization, and some of the most remarkable contributions to that civilization were made by the kingdom of Benin, which ruled the Niger Delta for more than 1,000 years.

Chapter 1 | "RULERS OF THE SKY"

A view of the Benin River in the present-day nation of Nigeria. This thickly forested region has for thousands of years been the home of the Edo people, farmers and warriors who founded the kingdom of Benin in A.D. 900.

The Niger River begins its majestic 2,600-mile course through West Africa in the mountains of Fouta Djallon on the Atlantic coast. From Fouta Djallon the Niger flows northeast into the rain-starved savanna. Reaching its northern limit at Timbuktu, the legendary center of African trade and learning, the river makes a wide bend to the south, forming a vast inland delta—when the rains finally fall in the summer months the river overflows its banks, turning the parched and tawny landscape into a green and fertile expanse where farmers can plant their crops and wandering herders can graze their cattle. The river then runs southeast, cutting across the lands of the Hausa and Yoruba and plunging from savanna country into dense tropical rainforest. At last, the Niger empties its waters into the Gulf of Guinea, forming another massive delta where numerous smaller rivers and streams meander through groves of squat, thick-rooted mangrove trees.

North of the coast, the landscape is dominated by massive 100-foot-tall trees, hanging vines, and thick undergrowth covering the forest floor. But this region of Africa is far from hostile to human life. The waters of the delta abound with fish, and the forest provides game for skillful hunters. The giant African snail also furnishes a ready source of protein. Palm trees yielding a nutritious oil grow wild here, as does the kola tree, whose nuts contain a highly prized stimulant. Natural clearings in the forest—often made by herds of elephants—provide farmers with fertile ground for the planting of

12

This striking mask, representing a water spirit, was carved by an artist who was a member of the Ijo people. Inhabiting the dense mangrove swamps of the Niger Delta, the Ijo were skilled at fishing; they traded part of their catch to the Edo of Benin in return for agricultural products such as yams.

crops such as yams. Thus it is not surprising that for at least 4,000 years the Niger Delta region has been home to several ethnic groups. Among these are the Edo—one of the most significant peoples in the history of the continent.

The Edo (also called the Bini) are closely related to the Yoruba, their northern neighbors. At some point in the past, the two peoples may have even inhabited the same territory. According to their own traditions, the Edo lived for a time at Ile Ife, the sacred center of Yorubaland. This is entirely plausible because the Edo and the Yoruba worship many of the same gods. Like the Yoruba, the Edo trace their origin to Olodumare, the creator god, who sent his son Oduduwa to Ile Ife, commanding him to create land upon the waters and populate the world with humans. A party of Edo hunters later ventured south from Ile Ife in search of land of their own. They established a new homeland on the western banks of the Niger, just above the delta.

For many centuries, the Edo lived in scattered villages without any form of central government. Each village was organized around clans, or descent lines. People who traced their family lineage to a common ancestor lived together in large compounds, adding new buildings as various family members married and had children. Each compound was headed by the oldest member of the clan. The head of the largest clan normally served as the chief of the village, with the elders of smaller clans serving as a council of advisers.

Throughout their early history, the Edo traded with other Africans—not merely their immediate neighbors but also those living in distant lands. In the challenging climate of Africa, people in a given region often found it difficult to supply all their needs, so they looked to other areas in order to supplement their diet. For example, many coastal fishing communities wished to obtain grains and cereals from the savanna, while savanna dwellers needed fish, meat, oil, and kola nuts. From earliest times, trade routes sprung up, linking the forestlands with the interior. Enterprising peoples, such as the Dyula of the western savanna and the Hausa of the central savanna, prospered by carrying goods back and forth along these routes. At the same time, the need to provide safety for travelers led to more complicated forms of political organization; scattered collections of villages gave way to larger states whose rulers saw to it that trade routes were free of bandits.

The Edo kingdom, which became known as Benin, dates back to A.D. 900, when a chief named Igodo took the title *ogiso*. (*Ogiso* means "ruler of the sky," an indication that the first kings sought to establish a link with Olodumare, thus giving their rule the sanction of the gods.) Little is known of Igodo's character or reign, but his son and successor, Ere, had a powerful impact on the development of Benin. The Edo chief Jacob Egharevba, in his *Short History of Benin* (first published in 1934), has described the achievements of Ere's rule:

> He was a lover of peace and concord. For instance, if there was fighting or quarrelling among his people a crier would be sent out by him to announce to the fighters the term *"A wua ne Ere"* meaning "quarrelling is forbidden by Ere" and at once peace would be restored. . . . He founded many villages . . . and the groups of craftsmen known as Onwina [carpenters] and Igbesamwan [carvers in wood and ivory]. . . . It was Ere who introduced the royal throne (*ekete*), the chief's rectangular stool (*agba*), the round leather fan (*ezuzu*), the round box (*ekpokin*) made of bark and leather, the swords of authority (*ada* and *eben*), beaded anklets (*eguen*) and collars (*odigba*), and a simple, undecorated form of crown. He also

13

A 19th-century engraving of a village on the banks of the Benin River. The Edo lived in isolated villages for many centuries before creating a centralized kingdom headed by rulers known by the title of ogiso.

14

introduced such domestic articles as wooden plates and bowls; mortars and pestles, which were carved by the Onwina; and the wooden heads, carved by the Igbesamwan, which are placed on ancestral shrines. Ere died peacefully after a successful reign.

The traditions of Benin account for 15 ogisos. The last ogiso, Owodo, was banished from the realm during the late 13th century because of various im-proper acts, including the execution of a pregnant woman. The elders of Benin could not agree on a new ogiso; instead, they appointed a man named Evian to run the government in a role similar to a modern president or prime minister. Evian governed successfully for a time, but when he attempted to act like a king and designate his son Ogiamwen to fol-low him, Benin entered a period of tur-moil in which a number of factions vied for power. Some of the Edo supported Evian; others insisted on a republican form of government in which there would be no king.

The solution to this conflict came from without. According to tradition, the Edo sent word to Ile Ife and invited Prince Oranmiyan, the son of Oduduwa, to rule Benin. Oranmiyan married an Edo woman, Erinmwinde, who soon gave birth to a son. "After some years of residence here," Chief Egharevba writes, "[Oranmiyan] called a meeting of the people and renounced his office, remarking that the country was a land of vexation . . . and that only a child born, trained and educated in the arts and mysteries of the land could reign over the people." Oranmiyan then returned to Ile Ife, but he left his son to rule in his place, and this son became known as Eweka I.

Though not all historians agree that Oranmiyan was the actual founder of a new dynasty in Benin, the Edo tradition accurately describes what became a defining event in the history of the kingdom: during the period of instability brought on by Evian's attempt to start his own dynasty, a powerful group from Yorubaland took advantage of Benin's weakness and imposed their will on the Edo. As the historian Basil Davidson has written, such political events were not unusual: "There is scarcely an African people without a more or less vivid tradition that speaks of movement from another place. Younger sons of paramount chiefs would hive off with their followers, and become paramount themselves in a new land. Stronger peoples would conquer those who were weaker, marry their women, merge with them, weave yet another strand in the fabric of African life." The developing saga of Benin, given new life by the arrivals from the north, proved to be one of the most dramatic in African history.

15

Chapter 2 | "LAND OF THE POWERFUL OBA"

This 17th-century engraving shows the oba of Benin (center, on horseback) accompanied by warriors, musicians, dwarfs, and leopards as he leaves the royal palace to attend a communal celebration. Benin's yearly religious festivals were the only occasions on which the oba was seen by his subjects.

Eweka I took the title *oba* when he began to rule Benin, and the obas were to reign in an unbroken line for nearly 700 years. According to Chief Egharevba, "Eweka had a long and glorious reign but he had many children who were always quarrelling among themselves. He sent some of them away to be chiefs (*enigie*) of famous villages. . . . Eweka I was the creator of Councillors of State or Kingmakers, afterwards known as *Uzama Nihinron*. . . . He made their titles to be hereditary and ordered that every Oba of Benin should be crowned by [them] . . . because it was they who sent to Ife to fetch Prince Oranmiyan." The uzama remained powerful throughout Benin's history, providing stability for its complex political system.

Other important traditions date from the reign of Oba Ewedo, Eweka's grand-son. Ewedo created posts for a number of royal officials, including the keeper of the oba's wardrobe, the recorder of deaths, and the keeper of the harem. He also took pains to enhance the personal prestige of his office, decreeing that only the oba could have a sword of state carried before him in the street and that all the Edo chiefs were to stand in his presence, so that only he remained seated in assem-blies. Ewedo began a number of building projects, including the royal palace and prison, which survived into the late 19th century.

Perhaps the greatest of all the obas was Ewuare, who came to the throne around the year 1440. In the Edo lan-guage, *ewuare* means "it is cool" or "the trouble has ceased," suggesting that the new oba was a man of peaceable nature. When his ambitions were aroused, how-

18

In this 19th-century sculpture of an oba, the ruler wears the traditional crown, collar, and beads associated with his office. In his left hand he carries a royal staff; in his right hand, he holds a ceremonial sword.

ever, he was far from docile. Ewuare's original name had been Ogun, and he was the son of Oba Orobiru, a capable ruler well loved by his people. As Chief Egharevba recounts, Orobiru's death touched off a violent sequence of events:

> The throne was vacant for several months because Ogun, the rightful heir, had been banished from the City with his younger brother, Uwaifiokun. It is said that Ogun sent Uwaifiokun to the City to find out whether the elders would like him to return home or not. Uwaifiokun, however, told the elders that he had not seen Ogun since their departure from the City, and he induced them to make him Oba, thus usurping the throne. Ogun therefore armed himself, and after lying in wait at the Oba's market at a ceremonial performance, murdered Uwaifiokun at night.

In spite of this bloody beginning, Ewuare proved to be an energetic and farsighted ruler. Like most successful African monarchs of the time, he was first and foremost a powerful military commander. His troops ranged far and wide into Yorubaland to the north and Igboland to the east, conquering more than 200 towns and forcing the local rulers to pay tribute to him. The Ekiti people of Yorubaland began to say of Ewuare, "The oba of Benin wages war on the earth below and [the god] Ogbomudu wages war in heaven." The neighboring Igbo now spoke of Benin as *Idu ala Eze ike,* "the land of the powerful oba."

With the wealth he gained from tribute, Ewuare expanded his capital, Benin City, building new roads and thoroughfares. As Egharevba relates, "It was he who had the innermost and greatest of the walls and ditches made round the City and he made powerful charms and had them buried at each of the nine gateways to the City, to nullify any evil charms which might be brought by people of other countries to injure his subjects." Much of the city was laid out in a grid pattern, with the streets running at right angles to one another. Some of the streets were as much as 120 feet wide, suitable for royal processions and other public spectacles.

Whereas Edo villages were organized mainly around descent lines, Benin City was divided into wards based on crafts and occupations. Thus blacksmiths would live in one ward, weavers in another, leatherworkers in a third. Within the wards, living space was divided into family compounds that were similar to those in the villages, with each compound being surrounded by a wall to define its boundaries. All the inhabitants of Benin City were considered retainers of the oba: that is, they lived under his protection, and their primary function was to provide for his needs and add to his glory.

The most formidable wall in Benin City loomed above the broad avenue that separated the oba's palace from the remainder of the city. This arrangement shielded the oba from public view and bolstered the belief that he was a sacred being gifted with powers of magic. (As in many West African kingdoms, the monarch's subjects were never allowed to see him performing ordinary human activities, such as sleeping and eating.) A number of ceremonies were designed to reinforce the aura surrounding the oba, and these were the only occasions on which he allowed himself to be seen by the people, who would come to the capital by the thousands from the surrounding countryside. Among the greatest occasions were the Igue festival, designed to reinforce the oba's spiritual powers, and the New Yam festival, celebrating the harvest. One of the most striking rites, according to Egharevba, commemorated an event from the time of Ewuare's exile:

> During the night, while [Ewuare] was resting under a tree, he felt something

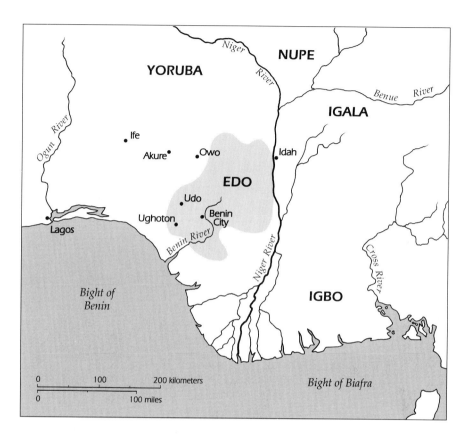

19

dripping on his head like water. In the morning he was greatly surprised to see it was blood, and on looking up he saw a leopard on the tree with blood dripping from its mouth. He got up hurriedly and then saw that he had been lying during the night on a snake. He killed both the leopard and the snake, and planted an *ikhimwin* tree on the spot, vowing that if ever he should become Oba of Benin he

A map showing the boundaries of Benin and the major ethnic groups of the lower Niger region.

20

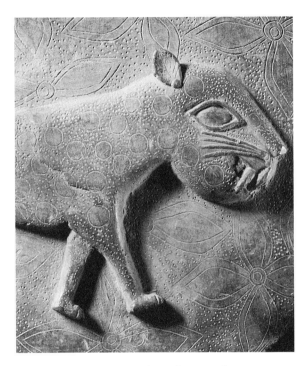

The head of a leopard from one of Benin's magnificent bronze plaques. Beginning with the reign of Ewuare the Great in the 15th century, the obas of Benin sacrificed a leopard each year to commemorate a miraculous event in Ewuare's early life.

would make it a place for worshipping the gods of his destiny. This vow he fulfilled by placing people there to watch the spot, and every year of his reign he sacrificed a leopard, and this example was followed by his successors.

Ewuare was aware that his personal aura alone could not sustain an expanding kingdom such as Benin. For this reason, he created the State Council to assist him in the process of governing. The State Council consisted of three distinct groups: the chiefs of the major towns; the palace chiefs, whose titles were created by the oba; and the powerful uzama, the six hereditary chiefs whose duty it was to install each new oba. Ewuare also took measures to establish an orderly succession to the throne. He created the title *edaiken* (crown prince) for his eldest son and appointed the edaiken to the State Council as an equal of the uzama.

Ewuare is credited with encouraging the art of carving wood and ivory, but in this area he was only continuing the great artistic tradition that had begun during the reign of Ere in the 10th century. Indeed, Benin had inherited a rich legacy that began with the vanished civilization now known as the Nok culture. As early as the 5th century B.C., the artists of the Nok culture—which flourished to the north of Yorubaland—were producing terracotta figures that rivaled the sculpture of ancient Greece. When the Nok culture died out around A.D. 200, the expertise of the Nok artists passed to the Yoruba, who produced astonishing lifelike heads for the sacred shrines of Ife.

Considering the close ties between Ife and Benin, it was only natural that the artists of Ife should export their skills to Benin City. The main work of Benin's artists was to sculpt the heads of deceased obas. The heads were displayed in funeral ceremonies and then placed in shrines, where current rulers could honor those who had previously held the throne. For three or four centuries the sculptors worked in wood or terra-cotta. Sometime during the 14th century, the art of working in bronze (a mixture of copper and tin) came to Benin by way of Ife.

In order to create their bronze sculptures, African artists employed a sophisticated technique known as the lost-wax method.

The artist would first make a clay model of the sculpture. When the clay dried, he would apply a thin layer of beeswax and carefully etch all the details of the sculpture into the wax. Then he would cover the wax with several more layers of clay, forming a thick mold. When the entire form was heated over a fire, the middle layer of wax would melt and drain off through the bottom of the form. At this point, the sculptor poured molten bronze into the top of the mold through a series of tubes. The bronze filled the space where the "lost" wax had been, conforming to all the fine details now baked into the surrounding clay. When the bronze cooled and set, the outer layers of clay were carefully broken, and the finished sculpture emerged.

21

The dramatic and expressive works produced by the Edo artists attest to the refinement of Benin's culture at a time when the kingdom had only limited contact with the peoples who lived beyond the forest belt and none at all with the world beyond Africa. By the time of Ewuare's reign, however, Europeans had already visited the western coast of Africa. When they reached the forestlands, they would help stimulate the artists of Benin to achieve their greatest period of creativity. But they would also bring ideas and practices that would ultimately cause the downfall of many African societies.

An early engraving shows Africans engaged in the art of metalworking. When the sophisticated technique of bronze casting reached Benin during the 14th century, the kingdom's artists began to produce magnificent sculptures in bronze.

Chapter 3 | WORLDS IN COLLISION

The top of this 17th-century bronze box is modeled after the roof of Benin's royal palace. The birds in the design represent the oba's magical powers, while the warriors bearing firearms indicate the growing importance of European weapons in the affairs of Benin.

Throughout the Middle Ages, which extended roughly from A.D. 500 to 1500, there was little outward difference between the kingdoms of Africa and the kingdoms of Europe—apart from the skin color of the people. On both continents, states were ruled by kings and queens whose power, in the eyes of their subjects, came directly from the Supreme Being. At the same time, a complex system of checks and balances operated in these states; monarchs ruled through the cooperation of local leaders—chiefs in Africa, barons in Europe—and many decisions were made by state councils rather than by the whim of an individual. Despite these similarities, Africans had no conception of Europe; the only light-skinned peoples they knew of were the Berbers of North Africa, who crossed the Sahara in great caravans to trade with the peoples of the savanna. Europeans, on the other hand, held a vague and generally alluring image of Africa as a mysterious and far-off land containing great riches, especially in gold, and fabulously wealthy kings such as Mali's Mansa Musa. Indeed, there were periods during the Middle Ages when Africa appeared to enjoy a level of prosperity far ahead of Europe's. During the 14th century, for example, when Europe was ravaged by the Black Death and the Hundred Years War, African empires such as Mali and Songhay were enjoying peace and prosperity.

Nevertheless, by the end of the Middle Ages, Europeans were sailing to the coast of Africa, whereas West Africans had yet to venture beyond the confines of their own continent. In later centuries, many Europeans would take this as proof of their racial superiority. However, to unbiased students of history, the varying fortunes of Europe and Africa indicate a far more complex set of causes.

Though political organization in both Africa and Europe appeared to have developed in a similar fashion, Europe's physical environment had always provided many advantages for its inhabitants. Early humans first discovered these advantages about 40,000 years ago when they developed the ability to make clothing and build shelters; this enabled hunting groups to migrate from Africa and other hot-weather regions, following game animals into colder climates. As William H. McNeill has written in his book *Plagues and Peoples*, "In leaving tropical environments behind, our ancestors also escaped many of the parasites and disease organisms to which their predecessors and tropical contemporaries were accustomed. Health and vigor improved accordingly, and multiplication of human numbers assumed a hitherto unparalleled scale."

Initially, moving to colder climates had drawbacks. Wild animals were less abundant, and humans found far fewer wild food plants than they had been used to in tropical climates. However, as McNeill points out, the absence of disabling diseases such as malaria and sleeping sickness allowed humans greater opportunity to find ways of altering their environment, "giving a much wider scope to cultural invention than had been attainable within the tighter web of life from which naked humanity had originally emerged." In other words, the challenge for Africans was adapting to their environment, which they had done brilliantly, evolving ways of life and thought that emphasized tradition, continuity, and balance. Europeans, on the other hand, had the opportunity to develop a restless, competitive outlook that would impel them to change their world.

By the Middle Ages, Europeans had learned to exploit their land to the fullest. They had adapted hand-held farming tools into the plow. Pulled first by oxen and then more efficiently by horses, the plow could cultivate far more land in a short time than could the muscle power of the African farmer, who was still using the iron-bladed hoe of his ancestors. Africans practiced hoe agriculture not

(Continued on page 29)

24

IMAGES OF ROYALTY

The art of sculpture in Benin dates back to A.D. 950, when Ere, one of the kingdom's first rulers, encouraged the creation of specialized guilds for craftspeople. Heirs to a great artistic tradition that began with the Nok culture in the 5th century B.C., Benin's artists displayed their mastery in a variety of materials, including wood, ivory, terra-cotta, and bronze.

A terra-cotta head from Benin. Working in terra-cotta required great skill because the sculpture had to be heated at exactly the right temperature; if the air inside the hollow mold became too hot, the resulting pressure would cause the figure to disintegrate.

This striking head dates from the early period of bronze casting in Benin (14th to 15th century). Sculptors created such heads to honor deceased obas; after being publicly displayed during funeral ceremonies, the sculptures would then be placed in a royal shrine.

A small ivory mask from 16th-century Benin, designed to be worn as a royal ornament. The mask itself portrays an oba, but the row of tiny heads adorning the oba's crown have Portuguese features.

This bronze head depicts a queen mother (iyoba). The queen mother, who had her own court and her own officers, played an important role in the affairs of Benin. Normally, the oba could depend on his mother for support, although Ose, a 19th-century iyoba, joined forces with the enemies of her son, Oba Obanosa.

(Continued from page 24)

A 16th-century woodcut depicts a European farmer plowing his fields. The use of plows drawn by oxen and horses led to increased food production and a rapid growth in Europe's population. Because of their expanding numbers, Europeans were driven to explore other lands.

because they lacked the intelligence of Europeans but because their environment allowed little innovation. For one thing, the presence of the tsetse fly, which transmits a deadly disease known as sleeping sickness, prevents the use of farm animals in many regions of Africa. Also, the tropical soil of Africa does not respond well to plowing, which causes plant-nourishing substances to wash away with the onset of the heavy summer rains. Even the growing of crops quickly exhausts the nutrients in tropical soils. For this reason, African farmers have for centuries planted fields for only 2 years running, after which they let them lie fallow for 10 years while they cultivate other fields. This system of land rotation has been adequate to sustain life in Africa, because the continent contains much land and a relatively small number of people. The rapidly expanding population of Europe did not have enough farmland to permit fallowing, so Europeans were compelled to experiment with new farming methods in order to survive.

In addition to their agricultural inventions, Europeans had also adapted the wheel to numerous uses. The most obvious of these was the transport of both goods and people. Equally important but now often unappreciated was the wheel's ability to transform the power of rivers and streams into mechanical energy. Much of Europe's abundant food supply resulted from the operation of mills whose grinding stones were driven by water wheels.

Africa's terrain, on the other hand—be it desert, wooded grassland, or dense tropical forest—made wheeled transport highly inefficient compared with the camel, the horse, the donkey, and human muscle power. Without wheeled vehicles, Africans had less opportunity to adapt the wheel to industrial uses.

The expansion of agriculture and industry brought about an age of prosperity in Europe. Population grew so rapidly that Europe was even able to rebound from the horrors of the Black Death, the 14th-century outbreak of bubonic plague that killed as much as one-third of the continent's people. By the 15th century, thriving and crowded Europe was ready to expand.

For centuries, Europe's prosperity had centered on the Mediterranean Sea, which linked Europeans with the Middle East and, through Middle Eastern merchants, the distant lands of India and China. Toward the end of the Middle Ages, Italian city-states such as Venice and Genoa controlled the Mediterranean, gaining vast wealth from their access to the goods of the East. The rulers and merchants of western Europe—Spain, Portugal, England, France, and Holland—desired above all to trade directly with India and China, bypassing the Mediterranean. They could accomplish this only by sailing around Africa.

For many decades, European navigators had plied the waters along the northwest coast of Africa, but they found that they could not proceed very far. Beyond the point where the Sahara gives way to the savanna, the winds blow from north to south all year long. Because the heavy, square-sailed vessels of the day could

This engraving of a caravel shows the sternpost rudder and one of the lateen (triangular) sails that made the caravel more maneuverable than any previous European craft. When Portuguese mariners acquired caravels during the 15th century, they were finally able to navigate the treacherous waters off the coast of West Africa.

31

sail efficiently only with the wind at their stern, any ship sailing down the African coast would stand little chance of returning. This assumption was proved conclu- sively in 1291 when Ugolino and Vadino Vivaldi, a pair of adventurous mariners from Genoa, boldly set off to sail around Africa. The intrepid Vivaldi brothers were sighted as they passed what is now Cape Dra on the coast of Morocco, but they were never seen again.

Not until the 15th century did anyone attempt to follow the Vivaldi brothers' example. By that time, European shipbuilders had adopted the lateen sail, a triangular sheet (used by Middle Eastern seamen since ancient times) that allowed ships to tack against the wind; they also followed Chinese shipbuilders by placing the ship's rudder in the stern rather than amidships, thus improving maneuverability. Finally, the seafarers of Portugal incorporated the lateen sail and the sternpost rudder into a new type of ship known as the caravel. A relatively lighter and more responsive vessel, the caravel could sail farther out from the African coast and thus pick up more favorable winds for the return journey. Once Portugal's ambitious mariners had a fleet of caravels at their disposal, Africans and Europeans were destined to encounter one another.

Beginning in 1446, when Nuno Tristão reached the Gambia River, the Portuguese gradually made their way south along Africa's Atlantic coast, establishing trade relations with a number of African peoples. By the 1470s they had reached the Gulf of Guinea and were exploring the bays now known as the Bight of Benin and the Bight of Biafra. They did not, however, make immediate contact with the kingdom of Benin because there were no Edo settlements near the coast. The coastal lands had been occupied since time immemorial by the Itsekiri and the Ijo, who traded fish and salt to the Edo in return for yams and other produce. The Itsekiri often acted as go-betweens (and occasionally rivals) in Benin's trade with the Portuguese.

Not until 1485 did a Portuguese emissary, João Afonso d'Aveiro, make the journey from the coast to Benin City. Oba Ozolua welcomed d'Aveiro and sent one of his leading officials, the chief of Ughoton, back to Portugal with the emissary to meet the king and discuss the opening of trade relations.

The surviving records of the era indicate that the Portuguese were highly impressed with the kingdom of Benin and looked upon its inhabitants as worthy partners in trade rather than inferior beings ripe for exploitation. For example, a letter of 1514 from King Manuel of Porugal to Oba Esigie makes forceful demands about the opening of certain markets but is couched in the most respectful language, as befitting a com-

(Continued on page 37)

SCENES FROM THE PALACE

During the 16th century, when European traders brought large amounts of copper and iron into Benin, Benin's sculptors were able to work on a grand scale. Using the same techniques they had employed to produce individual heads, the artists now created hundreds of decorative plaques that adorned the interior rooms and passageways of the royal palace in Benin City.

This 17th-century plaque depicts one of the drummers who made up Benin's corps of royal musicians. The floral designs in the background were inspired by patterns woven into Portuguese textiles.

An oba supported by two attendants. By casting the oba's legs in the form of mudfish, the artist expresses the Edo belief that the oba is the human counterpart of Olokun, the sea god.

Three hunters attack a leopard. Because the fierce jungle cat was so closely associated with the early life of Ewuare, the greatest of all the obas, it is featured in a number of Benin artworks. In addition, leopard-skin cloaks and necklaces made of leopards' teeth were highly prized items of apparel.

XVIII, 6.
98
1-15
31

This 17th-century plaque depicts an Edo chief whose high rank is indicated by the massive beaded collar he wears. The chief is accompanied by two heavily armed soldiers and a pair of musicians, one blowing a horn and the other playing a pair of wooden clappers.

(Continued from page 32)

munication between monarchs of equal stature:

> We have heard Dom Jorge, your ambassador, in all that he has said to us on your behalf. We were much pleased with his coming to us, so that from him we might learn of the goodwill which you profess touching our service. . . . Be assured that, because of our constant desire to further your interests, you may command and make use of all that is ours as though it were your own.

Esigie, who is remembered as one of the greatest obas, accommodated the Portuguese in their desire to trade for pepper, gold (mined by the Akan peoples of the forest belt), textiles, ivory, and slaves (many of them prisoners of war captured in the campaigns of Oba Ozolua). He also permitted some Christian clergymen to operate in Benin, teaching Portuguese and converting Africans to Christianity. (The influence of the Christian fathers, however, was not widespread—most of them died of malaria, to which many Africans had developed a natural resistance over the centuries.) In allowing missionaries access to his people, Esigie was no different from the rulers of many savanna states, who adopted and fostered the religion of Islam as a means of creating bonds with their North

37

This 16th-century ivory casket from Benin, created for European customers, dramatically portrays a pair of Portuguese soldiers. With their beards, pale skin, and prominent noses, the visiting Portuguese clearly appeared strange and rather sinister to Africans.

African trading partners. This contact between cultures was often beneficial to the savanna kingdoms, and the Portuguese presence was certainly a stimulus to the people of Benin. The most lasting evidence of that influence are the magnificent works of art produced by Benin artists, beginning with the reign of Esigie and lasting for the next 100 years.

Among the Benin masterpieces from this period are carvings in ivory, many of them depicting Portuguese visitors. Even more impressive are the ceremonial bronze plaques created by the lost-wax method and displayed in the numerous reception chambers and inner rooms of the oba's palace. Most of the plaques depict obas, palace guards, warriors, court musicians, and other members of the royal entourage. Previously, the output of Benin's artists had been limited by the scarcity of copper, which had to make its way to Benin from North Africa through overland trade routes. Once they could obtain large amounts of copper directly from the Portuguese ships, the Edo were able to work on a larger scale than ever

A pair of bowmen brandish their weapons in this dramatic bronze plaque. Benin's powerful army, the scourge of the lower Niger region, ensured that visiting Europeans would be on their best behavior while conducting business in the realm of the obas.

before and produce plaques by the hundreds. Some of the designs and techniques used in the plaques show that the sculptors adopted patterns common in Portuguese textiles and also studied the illustrations in European books.

When other Europeans learned of Portugal's profitable trade with West Africa, they were eager to follow suit. By the middle of the 16th century, the British and Dutch had made their way to the coast of Africa; being richer nations with more powerful navies, they were able to displace the Portuguese in many areas and take the lion's share of the African trade. Initially, the advent of new trading partners promised benefits for the Edo and other Africans. But before long, the interplay between Europe and Africa assumed a sinister and destructive nature.

39

Chapter 4 | THE SLAVE COAST

Throughout the 17th century, the people of Benin traded with British and Dutch merchants as equal partners. The trade developed to such an extent that the Edo devised sophisticated procedures to govern the trading process. In *Benin and the Europeans*, Alan Ryder describes these procedures:

> At the arrival of a ship at Ughoton [Benin's main port], the chief of that town dispatched a messenger to inform the Oba, as had been the practice in the sixteenth century. But instead of the Europeans being taken to Benin City, two or three *Iwebo* officials [palace chiefs] and twenty or thirty traders arrived to deal with them at Ughoton. . . . For their first visit to the Dutch merchants, the officials wore a dignified dress with strings of beads . . . around their necks. Kneeling they delivered salutations from the Oba, his mother and the three chief counsellors . . . presented some gifts of food in their name, and paid many compliments. Next they enquired after the state of the visitors' country, the progress of its wars and like subjects. Finally, after accepting a drink of spirits, they took ceremonious leave, without once mentioning questions of trade. . . . On subsequent days the officials returned in order to fix prices for any goods which had never been traded before; other items remained at the prices previously agreed upon. Keen bargaining ensued, sometimes lasting several weeks.

Those rare merchants who did have a chance to visit Benin City were impressed with the size of the capital, the arrangement of the streets, and the qual-

In this engraving, slaves are transported to a European ship anchored off the West African coast. By the mid–18th century, the transatlantic slave trade had taken a drastic toll on the societies of West Africa.

41

XXI.1

42

ity of the houses. One trader passed on the following account to Olfert Dapper, who included it in his *Accurate Description of the Regions of Africa:*

> At the gate where I went in on horseback, I saw a very big wall, very thick and made of earth, with a very deep and broad ditch outside of it. . . . Inside the gate, and along the great street just mentioned, you see many other great streets on either side, and these are also straight and do not bend. . . . The houses in this town stand in good order, each one close and evenly placed with its neighbor, just as the houses in Holland stand. . . . The king's court is very great. It is built around many square-shaped yards. These yards have surrounding galleries where sentries are always placed. I myself went into the court far enough to pass through four great yards like this, and yet wherever I looked I could still see gate after gate which opened into other yards.

Dapper's book appeared in 1668, but not more than a century later, the entire picture had changed. Europeans had begun to think of Africans as a lower order

This bronze plaque depicts an Edo trader of the 17th century. In his right hand, the trader holds a staff indicating his authority to conduct business on behalf of the oba; in his left hand he holds a manilla, a C-shaped metal bracelet used as currency in Benin's trading operations.

of humanity, and many West African societies had declined from their former grandeur. The driving force behind these dramatic changes was the transatlantic slave trade.

Slavery has existed in human society since ancient times, encompassing all parts of the world and all races, including the city-states of ancient Greece, the great kingdoms of Egypt, and the Roman Empire. Black Africans had enslaved one another long before they even knew that Europeans existed. Many of these slaves were prisoners captured in warfare; others had been convicted of serious crimes. Most often, the captives were incorporated into the armies or households of rulers or other powerful men—in a few cases, such as those of Kanem-Borno, the Akan states of the forest belt, and the larger city-states of Hausaland, slaves were also organized into communities of laborers. The trade between the savanna states and the Muslims of North Africa had always included a certain number of black slaves, desired by the Muslims as soldiers and household servants.

It was entirely natural, then, for Africans to offer captives to their European trading partners. But for the first 200 years of their dealings with Africa, Europeans' interest in buying slaves was outstripped by their desire for items such as pepper and ivory. The transatlantic slave trade would never have developed if not for the growth of European involvement in a distant part of the world—the Americas.

Beginning with the first voyage of Christopher Columbus in 1492, the nations of western Europe began to seize islands in the Caribbean Sea as well as great tracts of land in North and South America. Whereas in earlier years Europeans had voyaged to Asia and Africa to obtain spices and precious metals, they now found that these valuable commodities were theirs for the taking, once they had subdued the Indians of the New World. In order to establish gold and silver mines and plantations for crops such as sugar, however, the Europeans needed laborers, and the conquered Indian populations could not fill this need. Unused to such labor and prey to the diseases carried by Europeans, the Indians died in such numbers that in many parts of the New World their once-thriving populations all but disappeared.

Europeans soon realized that Africans could fill their needs for labor. Africans were strong and hardy, often skilled in

43

44

mining and tropical farming, and highly resistant to many diseases. Thus, as the economy of the New World expanded, European traders demanded more and more slaves from their African trading partners; captives began to play such a large part in the bargaining that Europeans soon referred to the lands bordering the Bight of Benin as the Slave Coast. By 1600, the total slave exports of West Africa had amounted to about 10,000 a year; by 1750 the annual total had risen to 100,000. All in all, during the entire duration of the transatlantic slave trade (1500–1900), about 12 million Africans were shipped from their homeland to the Americas. As Patrick Manning has pointed out in his 1990 book *Slavery and African Life,* the slave trade represented "the largest migration in human history to that time."

The slave trade had a powerful impact on the population of West Africa. Because many of the slaves were men in the prime of life, women began to outnumber marriageable men in many regions of Africa, and birth rates declined. Manning explains that although Africa's population may not have actually declined during the slave-trade era, it certainly did not grow. He calculates that in the normal course of events, the population of sub-Saharan Africa should have been 100 million by 1850, yet in fact it was only 50 million. During the same period, the populations of Europe and North America enjoyed substantial growth, and the wealth of both continents grew enormously, in large part because of African labor.

If population were the only way of judging the effects of the slave trade, Benin itself would not have suffered disastrously, at least compared with other areas of West Africa, such as Igboland and Senegambia. In 1789, for example, when British ships loaded 20,000 captives from Igboland in the eastern Niger Delta, they took only 1,000 from the ports of Benin. Most of that 1,000 would have been non-Edo who had been captured by Benin's army, and thus Benin itself would not have suffered severe population losses. However, as Benin's neighbors to the east and west grew wealthy from the slave trade and acquired firearms from the Europeans, the balance of power along the lower Niger shifted. Towns that had previously paid tribute to the obas ceased doing so, and their new firearms gave them the ability to raid Benin's territory and take on the more numerous Edo armies. Benin, along with many other African states,

A group of captives being transported overland by African slave traders. When the captives reached the coast, they were purchased by European merchants and loaded onto ships for transport to the Americas.

was forced to acquire firearms to maintain its military strength, and the Europeans, realizing their advantage, would only give firearms in exchange for slaves. The growing instability in the delta inevitably decreased the power of the obas and the prosperity of their kingdom.

In broader terms, the slave trade corrupted the society of Benin, just as it corrupted the society of every other African nation involved in it—no matter whether that nation was primarily selling slaves or losing its people to the slavers. Unlike other avenues of trade, the slave trade provided no wealth for African soci-

This copper sculpture from Benin depicts an Edo musketeer. By the 18th century, Benin and other African kingdoms were dependent on European firearms for defense against their enemies; they could obtain these weapons only by providing a steady supply of slaves in exchange.

46

ety. The money and goods exchanged for slaves remained in the hands of a narrow class of rulers and slave merchants. No benefits accrued to hardworking families as they did when textiles or other goods were exchanged; indeed, many families lost some of their most productive members without getting anything in return.

The Benin praised by Dutch visitors as late as the 1650s began to show a different face after only half a century of intense slaving. In 1700, for example, the Dutch merchant William Bosman wrote of Benin City, "Formerly this village was very thick and close-built, but now the houses stand like poor men's corn, widely distant from each other." As the historian Basil Davidson has pointed out, the art of Benin also began to decline in quality and sensitivity, and he links this change to the kingdom's political fortunes: "Moreover, this process of coarsening can be shown to have continued: the heads became clumsier and more gross in shape and feeling as the slaving years passed by and the old skills were overborne and set aside."

In light of all these factors, it is not surprising that European attitudes toward Africa began to change. In part, the change took place because those who profited from slavery felt the need to jus-

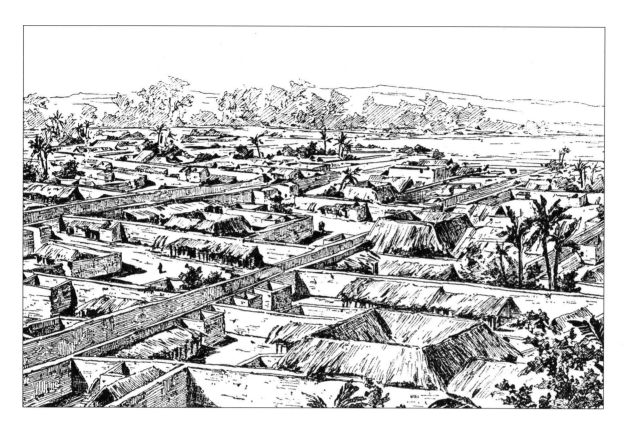

This engraving of Benin City was made by a British artist in 1897, when the once-grand capital of the obas had suffered greatly from the effects of war and political upheaval.

47

tify the exploitation and often unspeakably brutal treatment of so many human beings. If they could convince themselves (and others) that Africans were "backward" and "naturally servile," white slave traders and slave owners could even claim that they were providing these poor "savages" with a better life in the New World. And as the slave traffic progressed, the growing disparity in wealth between Europe and Africa—and the noticeable coarsening in African society—gave credence to European and North American feelings of racial superiority. Having once been an equal trading partner, Africa was now looked upon only as a ripe source of plunder. This drastic change would finally contribute to the overthrow of societies that had flourished for centuries.

Chapter 5 | "FAREWELL, FAREWELL!"

An Edo chief and two young hunters, photographed in the early 20th century. Though Benin was at this time part of the British empire, the Edo staunchly maintained their traditions and their pride.

By the beginning of the 19th century, the transatlantic slave trade became less profitable, due in part to the growing availability of cheap industrial labor in Europe and the Americas. The traffic in human beings in the Bight of Benin entered its final phase in 1809, when the British Parliament declared it illegal. The gradual decline of transatlantic slaving, however, was only the prelude to new forms of European exploitation.

In Benin and its surrounding territories, the British turned their attention to other goods, principally palm oil. Obtained from the nuts of the many palm trees growing wild in West Africa, palm oil was desired in Europe to lubricate machinery and for the manufacture of soap, candles, and margarine. The palm oil trade required the work of many individuals, who were needed to harvest the nuts, extract the oil, pour it into barrels, and transport the barrels to the ports for shipping. This commerce achieved such a scale that the British began to refer to the waterways of the Niger Delta as the Oil Rivers.

However, the Africans employed in the palm oil trade were not, in many cases, free laborers whose wages could usher in a new era of African prosperity. Europeans may have called a halt to slavery, but they had accustomed powerful men in Africa to profiting from their weaker neighbors, and this practice continued long after 1809. In many areas,

50

Workers harvest palm nuts to be used in the production of palm oil. After the abolition of the transatlantic slave trade in the early 19th century, palm oil became the major export from the coast of West Africa.

African rulers and slave merchants continued to take large numbers of captives. Instead of being sold to Europeans, the captives were now put to work along the Oil Rivers. In addition, black slaves were still in demand in North Africa, and the trans-Saharan slave trade continued unabated.

Now antislavery activists in Europe demanded the elimination of slavery within Africa. The British government in particular felt obliged—or believed it could be profitable—to act on these demands. In order to root out slavery completely, the British clearly needed to delve farther into the African interior. Before the 19th century, this had been largely impossible, because Europeans had virtually no resistance to malaria. (For many decades, Europeans referred to the African coast as "the white man's grave.") European slavers had mostly remained in their ships and relied upon African merchants to bring the slaves to the wharves. However, the development of the drug quinine in 1830 provided an effective treatment for malaria. The British could now push inland from the Niger Delta, both to search out illegal slavers and to further their commercial interests.

In 1849, the British established a consulship for the coastline of the Gulf of

Guinea, and in the ensuing years they steadily increased their influence in the region, forcing their will on Africans who resisted them. In 1885, the major European powers met in Berlin, Germany, and agreed on a plan to divide up Africa. According to this plan, the entire Niger Delta region was to become part of the British Empire, which by now included India and much of the Middle East.

In 1892, the British government persuaded the new oba of Benin, Ovonramwen, to sign a treaty by which he accepted the "gracious favor and protection" of Queen Victoria. In return the oba pledged, among other things, to have no dealings with other European powers, to grant wide authority to British consuls, to permit free trade between the British and other peoples in the delta, and to welcome Christian missionaries. Despite the one-sided nature of the treaty, the British government apparently intended to gain control over Benin in a gradual and peaceful manner. However, this was not the attitude of their main official in the area, Sir Ralph Moor.

An ambitious man, Moor wanted to advance his career by getting quick results in Benin. When the oba called a halt to trade in the delta because he was unhappy with the terms being offered, Moor saw an opportunity to create a confrontation. He dispatched his newly appointed deputy, James Phillips, on a mission to Benin City, with instructions to persuade the oba to lift his trade embargo. Phillips organized a party of eight Englishmen and numerous Itsekiri porters and set out for Benin in January 1897. Inexperienced in Africa, Phillips had little idea of the provocation he was creating.

While the Phillips party was en route, emissaries from Benin City informed them that the oba was taking part in the monthlong Igue festival and that he could not receive any visitors. Nevertheless, Phillips decided to follow his orders from Moor and press on. When Ovonramwen learned that the Englishmen were coming ahead, he ordered that they be given a peaceful reception. However, the war chiefs believed that Benin was being invaded by hostile forces, and they directed their troops to set up an ambush along the main road to the city. When the Phillips party approached, the Edo greeted them with a fusillade of rifle fire. Two men managed to escape into the forest and eventually made their way back to the coast. Phillips and the other six Englishmen died, either on the road or later in Benin City.

51

British troops firing on Edo troops during the final assault on Benin City in February 1897. Though the Edo defended their capital valiantly, their antiquated muskets were no match for the machine guns and artillery of the invaders.

52

When reports of the so-called Benin Massacre reached England, the public was outraged, and the government could no longer forestall the use of force. A squadron of British navy vessels, carrying detachments of soldiers and marines, was dispatched to the Benin River with instructions to take Benin City by force. The Edo did everything within their power to halt the advance of the British troops through the forest, and when this failed, they defended their capital with volleys of rifle fire and shells from the ancient cannon they had obtained many years earlier from the Portuguese. In the end, however, the outmoded weapons of the Edo were no match for the rapid-fire machine guns and powerful artillery pieces employed by the British. On February 18, 1897, the attackers mounted a final assault and captured Benin City.

Among the first acts of the conquerors was the looting of thousands of artworks from the royal palace and from nearby shrines. This action deprived the Edo of much of their artistic heritage and made it impossible for scholars in later generations to fully understand the development of Benin's world-class art. Reflecting on his countrymen's behavior in his 1982 book *City of Blood Revisited*, the historian Robert Home wrote: "For all their assumptions of racial superiority, the British at Benin did their best to destroy a remarkable artistic achievement, like the Mongols when they pillaged medieval Baghdad." Desecration was followed by destruction: a fire broke out on February 21, and by the time it had burned itself out, the royal palace and much of Benin City lay in ruins. As Home remarks, "The British always maintained that the fire at Benin was accidental, though the Edo never believed them."

Ovonramwen had fled the city before the final assault, and he remained a fugitive until August, when he surrendered to the British forces and was put on trial. The six war chiefs responsible for the ambush on the Phillips party were condemned to death. Two of them escaped execution by committing suicide, and a third was pardoned because of his youth. Ovonramwen himself was cleared of any involvement in the massacre and was offered the opportunity to continue as oba under British supervision, provided that he spend some time at the British colonial headquarters at nearby Calabar, where he would be instructed in the

Oba Ovonramwen wears a rueful expression as he sits on the deck of a British yacht in 1897, sailing into exile. He was obliged to remain in Calabar, a British outpost east of Benin, until his death in 1914.

53

ways of the British colonial system.

Believing that the British meant to keep him in Calabar, Ovonramwen fled again, going into hiding in the compound of an influential chief. However, after the British threatened the leading chiefs with death, they agreed to surrender their oba. This time the British

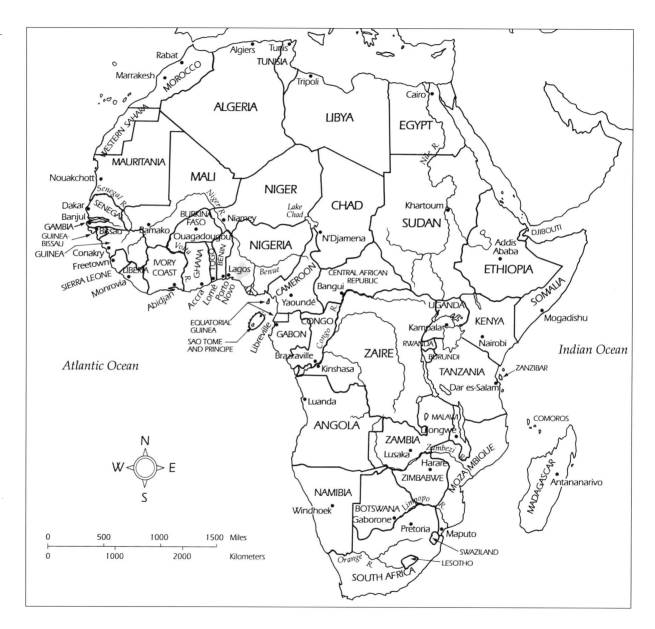

A map of present-day Africa. The shaded area indicates the former territory of the kingdom of Benin, now Bendel State in the nation of Nigeria.

54

sentenced Ovonramwen to permanent exile in Calabar, and he left his kingdom with sad and bitter words:

> I appeal to the Almighty and the Spirits of the departed Obas of Benin, my fathers, to judge between me and the Binis who ill-advised and cunningly sold me into the hands of the British troops. . . . Oh! Benin, Merciless and Wicked! Farewell, Farewell!

By the time of Ovonramwen's death in 1914, Benin had been incorporated into the larger British colony of Nigeria. The British preferred to govern their colonies by "indirect rule" through traditional leaders, and upon the death of Ovonramwen they appointed his son Aiguobasimi to be the new oba and restored him to Benin City. Aiguobasimi took the title Eweka II, forging a link with Eweka I, the first oba of the Oranmiyan dynasty in the 14th century. Eweka II rebuilt the royal palace on a smaller scale and reigned until his death in 1933, when he was succeeded by his son, Akenzua II.

When Nigeria obtained its independence from Britain in 1960, the Edo constituted one of the new nation's most important ethnic groups. Benin City became the capital of Nigeria's Mid-Western State, now known as Bendel State. (The modern nation of Benin, located just west of Nigeria, corresponds to the former state of Dahomey and has no relation to the former Edo kingdom.) Today, Benin City is a sprawling urban center with a population of more than 160,000. In the royal palace and the National Museum (erected in 1973), the remaining artworks from Benin's great periods of creativity are on display. Despite the many changes brought about by 20th-century technology and politics, the Edo continue to celebrate the Igue festival and the New Yam festival as their ancestors did. Their neighbors may no longer refer to Edo country as the "land of the powerful oba," but the Edo can proudly contrast their 1,000 years of imperial grandeur to the swift passage of the colonial empires that once imposed their will on Africa.

55

CHRONOLOGY

c. 2000 B.C.	Edo people migrate from central Nigeria to the Niger Delta region
A.D. 900	Kingdom of Benin emerges under Igodo, who takes the title *ogiso*
c. 950	Ere begins reign as ogiso; Benin's artists begin to carve in wood and ivory
late 13th century	Reign of ogisos comes to an end; Edo try republican form of government under Evian; Evian's ambitions cause political crisis
c. 1300	Edo send to Yorubaland for Prince Oranmiyan and invite him to become the ruler of Benin; Oranmiyan declines the throne, but his son, Eweka I, becomes the first *oba* of Benin
c. 1325	Reign of Oba Oguola begins; bronze-casting techniques come to Benin from Yorubaland
1355–80	Reign of Oba Ewedo, who creates new posts for royal officials and undertakes numerous building projects
1440–73	Reign of Ewuare the Great, who increases the wealth and power of Benin by military conquest and expands the capital, Benin City; Portuguese mariners begin to explore the Atlantic coast of West Africa

1485	Portuguese emissary João Afonso d'Aveiro visits Benin City; Oba Ozolua sends ambassador to Portugal
1504–50	Reign of Oba Esigie, who fosters trade and cultural relations with Portuguese; art of Benin enters its golden age as sculptors produce hundreds of bronze plaques for the royal palace; British and Dutch begin to replace Portuguese as trading powers in West Africa
1650–1850	Traffic in slaves dominates relations between Europeans and West Africans; millions of Africans are shipped to the Americas; Benin and other African societies begin to decline; Europeans develop racist views of Africa
early 19th century	British Parliament outlaws slave trade; palm oil trade replaces slaving in commerce between Benin and Britain
1849	British establish consulship for Gulf of Guinea and extend their influence in Benin
1892	Oba Ovonramwen signs treaty that further expands British power in Benin
1897	British delegation is ambushed en route to Benin City; British forces retaliate by occupying Benin City and exiling Ovonramwen; kingdom of Benin ceases to exist
1960	Nigeria gains independence; Benin City becomes capital of Mid-Western (now Bendel) State

FURTHER READING

Connah, Graham. *African Civilizations*. Cambridge: Cambridge University Press, 1987.

Dark, P. J. C. *Introduction to Benin Art and Technology*. Oxford: Clarendon Press, 1973.

Davidson, Basil. *Africa in History*. Rev. ed. New York: Collier, 1991.

———. *The African Genius*. Boston: Little, Brown, 1969.

———. *The African Slave Trade*. Rev. ed. Boston: Little, Brown, 1980.

Davidson, Basil, with F. K. Buah and the advice of J. F. A. Ajayi. *A History of West Africa, 1000–1800*. New rev. ed. London: Longmans, 1977.

Egharevba, Jacob. *A Short History of Benin*. 3rd. ed. Ibadan: Ibadan University Press, 1960.

Forde, Daryll, and P. M. Kaberry, eds. *West African Kingdoms in the Nineteenth Century*. Oxford: Oxford University Press, 1967.

Freyer, Bryna. *Royal Benin Art*. Washington, D.C.: Smithsonian Institution Press, 1987.

Gimpel, Jean. *The Medieval Machine: The Industrial Revolution of the Middle Ages*. New York: Penguin, 1976.

Hodgkin, T. H. *Nigerian Perspectives: An Historical Anthology*. Oxford: Oxford University Press, 1975.

Home, Robert. *City of Blood Revisited: A New Look at the Benin Expedition of 1897.* London: Rex Collings, 1982.

Hull, Richard W. *African Cities and Towns Before the European Conquest.* New York: Norton, 1976.

McEvedy, Colin. *The Penguin Atlas of African History.* New York: Penguin, 1980.

McNeill, William H. *Plagues and Peoples.* New York: Anchor, 1976.

Manning, Patrick. *Slavery and African Life.* Cambridge: Cambridge University Press, 1990.

Oliver, Roland, and Brian M. Fagan. *Africa in the Iron Age.* Cambridge: Cambridge University Press, 1975.

Park, Mungo. *Travels in the Interior Districts of Africa.* Reprint of the 1799 edition. New York: Arno Press / New York Times, 1971.

Ryder, A. F. C. *Benin and the Europeans, 1485–1897.* New York: Humanities Press, 1969.

Shaw, Thurstan. *Nigeria: Its Archaeology and Early History.* London: Thames and Hudson, 1978.

Smith, Robert. *Warfare and Diplomacy in Pre-Colonial West Africa.* 2nd ed. Madison: University of Wisconsin Press, 1989.

UNESCO General History of Africa. 8 vols. Berkeley: University of California Press, 1980–93.

Webster, J. B., and A. A. Boahen, with M. Tidy. *The Revolutionary Years: West Africa Since 1800.* New ed. London: Longman, 1980.

GLOSSARY

bronze
a metal created by the combination of copper and tin; used by Benin artists to create numerous sculptures

caravel
a light, maneuverable sailing vessel developed by Portuguese shipbuilders during the 15th century

delta
a wide, flat plain, usually at the mouth of a river, covered by a network of waterways

edaiken
title used by the crown prince of Benin

Edo
black African people who created the kingdom of Benin; one of the major ethnic groups of Nigeria

Igue festival
monthlong rite through which the oba of Benin increases his spiritual powers

lost-wax method
technique of metal casting with which Benin artists created bronze sculptures

malaria
deadly parasitic disease transmitted by various mosquitoes; common throughout the West African forest belt

Middle Ages
period of European history extending roughly from 500 to 1500

missionary
one who attempts to spread the teachings of a particular religion among people who observe a different religion

oba	title used by the rulers of Benin since 1300
ogiso	title used by the rulers of Benin between 900 and 1300
palm oil	oil obtained from the nuts of African palm trees; important trade item during the 19th and early 20th centuries
sleeping sickness	a deadly parasitic disease transmitted to both humans and animals by the tsetse fly, which breeds throughout the West African forest belt
transatlantic slave trade	traffic in human beings that lasted roughly from 1500 to 1900 and resulted in the shipment of 12 million Africans from their homeland to the Americas
uzama	hereditary Edo chiefs who have the responsibility of crowning the oba

61

INDEX

PHILIP KOSLOW earned his B.A. and M.A. degrees from New York University and went on to teach and conduct research at Oxford University, where his interest in medieval European and African history was awakened. The editor of numerous volumes for young adults, he is also the author of *El Cid* in the Chelsea House HISPANICS OF ACHIEVEMENT series and of *Centuries of Greatness: The West African Kingdoms, 750–1900 in Chelsea House's* MILESTONES IN BLACK AMERICAN HISTORY series.

PICTURE CREDITS

Photocopy by J. Beckett: p. 14 (neg. #2A21318), p. 47 (neg. #2A21319); The Bettmann Archive: p. 29; Bridgeman Art Resource, NY: p. 28; British Museum, London: p. 21; Courtesy Department Library Services, American Museum of Natural History: p. 48 (neg. #14041), p. 50 (neg. #14063); Photographs by Bruce Fleischer, Jeffrey Ploskonka, Franko Khoury, National Museum of African Art, Eliot Elisofon Photographic Archives, Smithsonian Institution: pp. 18, 38, 46; General Research Division, The New York Public Library: p. 53; The Illustrated London News Picture Library: p. 52; Library of Congress: p. 31; The Schomburg Center for Research in Black Culture, The New York Public Library, Astor, Lenox and Tilden Foundations: pp. 16, 40, 45; Aldo Tutino Art Resource, NY: p. 26; The Werner Forman Archive Art Resource, NY: pp. 2, 8, 10, 12, 20, 22, 25, 27, 33, 34, 35, 36, 37, 42.
Maps by Gary Tong: pp. 6, 19, 54.